HOECK

BERLIN PUB TRADITION
since 1892

Matthias Gerschwitz

HOECK

BERLIN PUB TRADITION
since 1892

Wilhelm Hoeck 1892:
Stories and histories from the
oldest beer pub in Berlin-Charlottenburg,
home of a 1932 Olympic champion.

AUTHOR

Matthias Gerschwitz, born 1959, was raised in Solingen, a German town between Cologne and Düsseldorf. After his university graduation, he worked as product manager for a manufacturer of household products and subsequently for an international fragrance company. He moved to Berlin in 1992 where he has been working as a marketing consultant. He started publishing books in 2007, initially focusing on his fondness for history.

Bibliographic information published by the Deutsche Nationalbibliothek

The Deutsche Nationalbibliothek lists this publication in the Deutsche Nationalbibliografie; detailed bibliographic data are available on the internet: http://dnb.dnb.de

© 2018 Matthias Gerschwitz | www.matthias-gerschwitz.de
based on »Molle und Medaille« (German edition)
Translation: Matthias Gerschwitz & Vivian Romney
Cover, Layout, Typesetting: Matthias Gerschwitz | Illustrations: Bernd Zeller
Published and printed by BoD- Books on Demand, Norderstedt | ISBN: 978-3-7528-5445-9

TABLE OF CONTENTS

Wilhelm Hoeck 1892
Wilmersdorfer Straße 149 · 10585 Berlin/Germany
Telephone: +49 30 341 81 74 · www.wilhelm-hoeck.de

STEP IN, PLEASE!

Following the traces of an old city usually means discovering the city center. But if you want to get a whiff of the famous *Berliner Luft* – the »Air of Berlin«, as a well-known Berlin operetta song from 1904 is called –, there are many places to explore. Berlin as it is today did not exist before October 1, 1920. The first German megacity emerged from the former royal residence first mentioned in the 13th century, seven other cities, fifty-nine villages and twenty-seven other rural districts. Many of the historic ninety-six boroughs are still alive. This is why the Berlin feeling is connected to typical Berlin attributes rather than architecture. Berlin in essence is characters, like the organ grinder who delights the audience with old Berlin melodies. It is the infamous *Schnauze mit Herz* Berlin way to talk, meaning »attitude with a big heart«. It is the *Milljöh* – the social environment of the poor living in the backyards of tenements around 1900 and the many beer taverns located at almost every other street corner.

Today, not many Berlin originals remain. Only a few organ grinders keep memories alive; most of the backyards are redeveloped; instead of the *Berliner Schnauze* dialect you hear languages and dialects from near and far. And many taverns have given way to upscale bars, restaurants and lounges. Some of them do look old, but mostly are nothing more than window dressing. But some real historic taverns are still to be found, places that seem to have been there ever since man first set foot into what later became known as *Berlin*. You may have to search for those places, since they are not necessarily located on worn tourist itineraries. But this exactly why the visit is worth the detour.

Wilhelm Hoeck (1870 – 1933)

This book is about such a gem of Berlin gastronomy: the old-style Berlin pub and restaurant *Wilhelm Hoeck 1892* in Berlin-Charlottenburg, not too far away from the opera house *Deutsche Oper*. Just enter, and you will be captivated by a long gone era. You forget time and plans, and stay until the last call and glass. And you will hear yourself promise to come back and show it to all your friends. Many have kept their word. No wonder: once you have been to *Hoeck*, you are compelled to return as often as possible. *Wilhelm Hoeck 1892* is old and antique, original and authentic. Dark paneled walls, scoured tables, time-honored schnapps kegs and shelves full of old bottles tell stories and histories from more than onehundred twenty-five years. It sure is a fine piece of old Berlin.

OUTSIDE BERLIN'S GATES

The »fine piece of old Berlin« actually is a fine piece of old Charlottenburg, which still was a city in its own rights when Wilhelm Hoeck started his business in 1892.

According to documents from 1239, today's Charlottenburg was first mentioned as the colony of *Lucene*. Later, names like *Lützow, Lützen* or *Lietzow* appeared. The colony was located south of the *Spree* river, close to the actual Charlottenburg's town hall. Since 1937, a street named *Alt-Lietzow* recalls the origins of the name.

Sophie Charlotte, wife of *Frederick III, Elector of Brandenburg*, must have fallen in love with this particular landscape when she decided to have *Lietzenburg Palace* built.

Charlottenburg Palace (around 1900)

All the craftsmen working on the building between 1695 and 1699 needed somewhere to live. So, a little colony was built just across the construction area.

In 1701, the *Elector of Brandenburg* was crowned Prussian King *Frederick I*, and *Sophie Charlotte* ordered the *Lietzenburg Palace* to be upgraded to a representative place. When she died in 1705, Frederick renamed the palace and the colony as Charlottenburg to honor his beloved wife. The colony received its town charter. Although the king had the palace completed, he never set foot into the building, but continued to mourn in the *Berlin Stadtschloss* palace.

His successor, *Frederick William I*, also known as the *Soldier-King,* did not really care for *Charlottenburg Palace,* but did invest in enlarging the town. His son, *Frederick II,* known as *Frederick the Great*, did not follow the tradition of his predecessors. He relocated the royal court to Charlottenburg and added prestigious buildings to the steadily growing town. *Frederick the Great* later left Charlottenburg for his newly built *Sanssouci Palace* at Potsdam. But his successors on the Prussian throne returned and made Charlottenburg their favorite residence.

Meanwhile the townspeople of Berlin also were attracted to the Western suburb; it became a favorite destination for weekends and summer vacations. No wonder, as of 1770 many restaurants and beer gardens opened along the main streets *Charlottenburger Chaussee* and *Berliner Straße* – today: *Straße des 17. Juni* and *Otto-Suhr-Allee*. They led from *Brandenburg Gate* through the *Tiergarten* forest into the heart of Charlottenburg. As of 1817, a regular boat line on the Spree river also connected the two cities. This was too expensive for most of the citizens. They preferred carriages, the so-called *Torwagen* – an early and uncomfortable form of public transportation. Later, a savvy entrepreneur offered a regular service with well-sprung carriages named *Kremser* after their inventor, which operated up to 40 times a day. They were replaced by horse-drawn streetcars in 1865. In 1881, finally, the first electric streetcars connected Charlottenburg to the Berlin city limits at the *Brandenburg Gate*.

But not only leisure activities attracted the Berlin's citizens. Charlottenburg became an sought after place to live, because estates were less expensive than in Berlin. Subsequently, wealthy bankers and entrepreneurs like *Werner von Siemens* built representative mansions with park-

»Berliner Straße« (around 1800), direction Charlottenburg Palace

like gardens. By the way: on March 1, 1879, the *von Siemens* mansion became the first private building in Germany to be illuminated by electric light.

As the entrepreneurs moved to Charlottenburg, they also relocated their companies, such as the *Royal China Manufactory KPM* or *Siemens*. The steadily rising tax receipts allowed the town to grow from a residential suburb to an upscale town with broad streets, well-groomed parks, splendid residences and impressive public buildings. The new jewel in the crown was the *Kurfürstendamm*, which before had been nothing more than a riding path to the *Hunting Lodge* at the *Grunewald* forest. But starting in 1890, the *Kudamm*, as it is still fondly called, became a swank boulevard flanked by baronial estates even in its side streets. It was a place to promenade and display one's wealth and a place to live life to the fullest, to enjoy art, culture and all forms of entertainment. And there were many places to go: an opera house, several theaters, and cafés and restaurants that opened almost every other month.

But the heart of Charlottenburg still beats in the historic center around the *Wilmersdofer Straße*, which leads straight through the middle of town. A walk along the street lets you explore the development of Charlottenburg. The southern area between *Adenauerplatz* and the railroad bridge is part of the *Kurfürstendamm* area. The middle part up to *Schillerstraße* today is a shopping mile with a mall, department and consumer electronic stores and many small retailers. It once used to be a busy main street with a lot of traffic, until it was converted to a pedestrian area in 1978. North of the intersection with *Bismarckstraße* it is a typical working class Berlin neighborhood, and this is where you find *Wilhelm Hoeck 1892*.

When the construction of the *Charlottenburg Palace* started in the early 17th century, the Prussian master-builder *Eosander von Göthe* (not to be confused with the famous poet laureate *Johann Wolfgang von Goethe*), built so-called Baroque style model houses for the craftsmen. Three buildings still exist:

The oldest preserved dwelling was built in 1712 and is located at *Schustehrusstraße 13* and today houses a museum for pottery. It was almost illegally torn down in 1983, but the public intervened. Shortly after, it was restored to its original appearance using original material and craftsmanship.

The small timbered house at *Wilmersdorfer Straße 18* was built around 1720. After originally being a private home, the owner later opened a beer pub in 1900. Twenty-six years later a motorcycle dealership moved in. After that, automobiles were sold. In summer 2006, a wine restaurant opened on the premises. Currently, it accommodates a wine tasting school.

The »youngest« of the three houses is located at *Haubachstraße 8*. Although built a hundred years later than the other ones, it matched the Baroque style model buildings exactly. Today, it is private property.

1960 | *Charlottenburg, Baroque building (1712), Schustehrusstraße 13* | 2008

1935 | *Charlottenburg, Baroque building (1720), Wilmersdorfer Straße 18* | 2008

1960 | *Charlottenburg, Baroque building (1816), Haubachstraße 8* | 2008

Presumably, all houses in this area once looked like these three. With a steadily growing population, more housing space became essential. The little model houses gave way to two- and three-story buildings. With the building boom of the end of the 19th century, they were replaced by four- and five-story buildings. For those interested in architecture, the intersection of *Wilmersdorfer Straße* and *Haubach-straße* mirrors all building styles between 1720 and 1920.

When the German Empire was founded in 1871, Charlottenburg counted 20,000 inhabitants with a steadily increasing population. In 1893, the number jumped over the 100,000 mark and in 1920, when Charlottenburg was incorporated into Berlin, there were more than 325,000 people living within the limits of the newly formed 7th District. Today, as of December 31, 2017, the population numbers to some 339,000 people.

THE »WILHELM HOECK« STORY

What happened in 1892? The escalator was patented in the U.S. while the preserving jar was invented in Germany. The theater at *Schiffbauerdamm* in Berlin opened its gates; some Berlin painters and sculptors created the art group *Secession*, and sports fans celebrated the formation of *Hertha BSC Berlin*, one of the major league soccer clubs that still exists in the German capital.

Wilhelm Hoeck, born on December 22, 1870 as the son of a farmer, had just come of age. He was young, ambitious and driven by the desire to become a successful business-man. So he opened a wine store in Charlottenburg, which soon relocated to a newly built house at *Wilmersdorfer Straße 149*. The building belonged to a commercial paint-

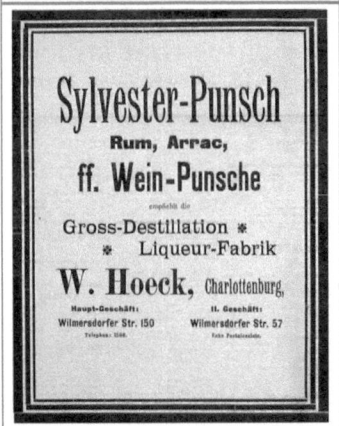

Newspaper ads (1901)

ing company that occupied the left side of the ground floor, while Hoeck took the store on the right. The salesroom was big enough to establish a tasting room, a novelty for Berlin wine stores in those days. But that was not enough for Hoeck. In 1896, he expanded his business to a second location across from *Charlottenburg Palace* and started distilling schnapps and cordials. Obviously, he recognized the dynamics of the market; the production premises soon were bursting at the seams. Hoeck had to find bigger premises, and by fortunate coincidence something came up in the direct neighborhood of his store. In 1900, he moved his production facilities to *Wilmersdorfer Straße 150.* He also opened a second wine store three blocks south. But after a year, he had to close the additional store, as it did not pay off.

With an established and successful business, Hoeck set his sights on fulfilling his personal plans. On May 9, 1900 he walked down the aisle of the Charlottenburg *Luisenkirche,* (named after another Prussian queen), with Margarete Böhnert, daughter of a local industrialist. They were to raise three children: Ilse (born November 9, 1901), Kurt (born November 21, 1902) and Horst (born May 19, 1904). As typical for the Wilhelmian time, Margarete took care of household and children, while the family head dedicated his energy to the company's constant growth. In 1911, he succeeded in acquiring the property *Wilmersdorfer Straße 149,* where his store was located, and immediately began to remodel. The office space of the former owners was converted into the wine store. The tasting area was enlarged

Margarete Hoeck with Horst (left), Kurt und Ilse (front)

to a tavern with a huge bar and a kitchen. The company's office was placed at the rear building, and the distillery disappeared to the basement underneath the two rear-yards. The family took up residence in a huge flat on *bel étage*. Wilhelm Hoeck certainly brought home the bacon:

he was a successful entrepreneur, owned a both commercial and residential real estate and was becoming a distinguished member of the Charlottenburg society.

Every morning at ten o'clock Wilhelm Hoeck entered his pub, which had opened three hours earlier. His first duty was to pan the room and look for guests that were tipsy or even already drunk. They would have to leave, because he expected the entrepreneurs, store-owners and executives from the companies nearby for a late breakfast at a regular's table. Hoeck wanted to impress his upper-class guests with a refined and respectable atmosphere.

Nevertheless, the district north of *Bismarckstraße*, where *Wilhelm Hoeck 1892* was located, was a more working class district. So, the afternoons and evenings were reserved for the working class people living in the neighborhood to enjoy their share of *Molle* (beer) and *Korn* (schnapps) after a hard day's work. They had to be home for supper, but returned afterwards or sent their sons over to buy another beer to bring home. So, the boys from the neighborhood were trained early to become future *Hoeck* regulars.

Window display (around 1910)

Wilhelm Hoeck was a patriarch, a typical entrepreneur of his time. He supervised the waiters' work from a standing desk aside, or he was enthroned at the huge copper cash register, which commanded the guests' respect as much as the man himself. The employees knew: cheating was not allowed. No doubt, the business flourished. Hoeck did not only sell his products at his pub, but also delivered schnapps and cordials to many taverns and private households throughout the greater Berlin area. Keep in mind, that around 1910 there were more than three hundred distilleries and liquor producing companies in Berlin alone! Obviously, the Hoeck business had excellent references. And its schnapps and liquor creations were of superb quality.

Kurt & Horst Hoeck (around 1910)

Hoeck delivered his products with horse-drawn wagons for which he has built a depot in the rear-yard. The whole family was passionate about horses. The children took riding lessons, and Wilhelm Hoeck was a regular visitor at the Berlin-Mariendorf racetrack that had opened in 1913. So, it was not surprising, that Hoeck started distilling a special cordial named *Traber* (trotter).

After 1918, reparation payments from WW I led to a galloping inflation which climaxed in November 1923. In that particular month, the exchange rate of 1 US-Dollar rose to astronomic 4.2 trillion Reichsmark. Gustav Stresemann, who has been elected German Chancellor in August 1923, managed to organize a monetary reform, which halted the inflation, but he had to call for a vote of confidence two months later. In those days, there was not much confidence in politics, politicians or economic upswing. Many Germans thought about emigration. One of them was Oskar Rüttler, Ilse Hoeck's fiancé. The merchant from Frankfurt/Oder was eager to seek his fortune in South America, and Ilse was willing to share the adventure. They married on January 22, 1924 and left Berlin shortly afterwards for Argentina.

After overcoming inflation, Germany's economy slowly but steadily bounced back to normality, a phase of consol-

Letterhead (1928)

idation began. Wilhelm Hoeck was looking ahead and started to invest in his business. First, he updated the distillery. In 1926, he replaced the old bar from 1911 with a new and functional one. He also installed a brand new tapping system, which still does duty today. Although it has more than 90 years on the clock, it still looks contemporary. That is a benefit of the clear and straight *Bauhaus* design style, which assumed that form follows function.

Both Hoeck sons completed a business education. First-born Kurt was supposed to step into his father's shoes, while younger son Horst pursued his athletic endeavors. But 1930 all plans had to be changed. Only a few days after his 28th birthday, Kurt died. The official cause of death was accidental gas poisoning, but in truth, Kurt committed suicide together with his girlfriend, whose parents would have never accepted a barkeeper's son as their son-in-law. But the church refused burial to suicides, and the

Hoeck family was very devout. So, Wilhelm Hoeck and the congregation agreed upon the purchase of a family burial place in return for an inconspicuous cause of death.

With Kurt's death the family business had to be reorganized. Horst, who was an enthusiastic athlete, had to be groomed to take over the family business. Since the early

Hoeck family grave

1920s, he had been active in rowing; he had been German champion for several times, had taken part in the 1928 Olympic Games in Amsterdam, and he was member of the Germany's 1932 team for the Los Angeles Olympics. There he crowned his career with a Gold medal in the coxed four. But only a few months later, both his parents died in short succession. So, he abandoned his rowing career and started a new life as the owner of a wine store, a distillery and a pub. Although he was an athlete at heart, he managed to keep the business. It was his iron will and the Prussian virtue of dedication to duty that bestowed success on him. *It is always time for a drink* was a common saying in those days, and the political changes, that had taken place, justified or sometimes even enforced an additional beer or schnapps.

Since January 30, 1933, the National Socialists formed the German government, and no one was unscathed. In 1934, the NS party requisitioned rooms in the Hoeck building for three local groups just to move out a few months later. But that did not harm the business success. Horst Hoeck took care of the schnapps and liquor production while Erich Emanuel, who had joined the company in 1922 as 15-year old apprentice, managed the pub and the store. But despite work, Horst Hoeck had enough spare time to date young ladies every now and then. He was elegant and well-mannered, and had a wide circle of acquaintances. A friend introduced him to a young actress by the name of Margot Ruth Lücken. They fell in love and married 1937.

Letterhead (1934)

Wilhelm Hoeck
LIKÖRFABRIK ✦ WEINGROSSHANDLUNG

BANK-KONTO DEUTSCHE BANK DEP-KJ
BERLINER STADTBANK GIRO-KASSE 101

POSTSCHECKKONTO BERLIN NR. 108321
FERNSPRECHER AMT C 4 WILHELM 1506

CHARLOTTENBURG
WILMERSDORFERSTRASSE 149

GEGRÜNDET 1892

Two years, later they announced the birth of their daughter Karin. But the marriage was troubled and they divorced in 1941. Margot Lücken died only one year later.

In 1942, Horst Hoeck celebrated his second marriage. In the famous Berlin *Kaiser-Wilhelm-Gedächtniskirche* (Emperor William Memorial Church) he exchanged wedding vows with Ingrid Patermann, whose father owned the food company *Bio-Malz* located in Teltow outside of Berlin. Three children resulted from the marriage: Myro, Horst jr. and Barbara.

Ingrid's older brother was supposed to inherit the *Bio-Malz* company, but he was killed in action. So, Horst Hoeck had to fill the void. His father-in-law asked him to close the Hoeck company including the tavern. But Horst was clever enough to keep the family business alive by installing the employee Erich Emanuel as general manager. Little did he know how wise this decision would turn out to be!

In 1942, Horst Hoeck and his wife moved into a house in the village of Kleinmachnow, situated between Berlin and Teltow. Hoeck joined *Bio-Malz* as director, a position he would hold until postwar times.

In 1945, Germany was divided into four military zones, and the *Bio-Malz* company was located in the Soviet Zone. Contrary to the Western occupying forces, the Soviets looked early for politically unburdened Germans to rebuild the administration. Horst Hoeck was part of their plans. In 1947, he was offered the position as head of the foodstuff, drinks and tobacco department for the Soviet Zone, but he refused. Filled with indignation, he said: »*I am not a Communist!*« This was true, but awkward, and, as he admitted later, impetuous. After having been courted for some time by the Soviets, he suddenly was suspected of embezzlement. A propaganda trial was to be set up, and the verdict was quickly rendered: the death penalty. Before he went to court, there were endless interrogations. When left alone for a moment, he attempted to escape by jumping out of a window on 3rd floor, severely injuring himself. He had to be taken to a military hospital. Soon it became clear that he needed the care of a civil hospital. That mobilized Ingrid Hoeck into action.

Dr.-Ing. Horst Hoeck, Ingrid and Horst's son, remembers the unbelievable feat: Ingrid Hoeck finally had convinced the district attorney to agree to transferring her husband to a civil hospital. On the day scheduled, she drove up to the military hospital in a West-Berlin ambulance, pretending she was ordered to pick up the injured prisoner. Doctors and nurses did not notice the deceit and moved the guerney into the ambulance, which left the premises at high speed and with flashing lights and a wailing siren. By the time the military ambulance arrived at the hospital, Ingrid and Horst Hoeck had already reached the British sector of Berlin.

Although it had been clear that they would not remain in the Soviet zone, Ingrid Hoeck had only managed to transfer the bare necessities from Kleinmachnow to Charlottenburg. Many personal items had been left behind, among them the 1932 gold medal, which was kept in a safe.

But even Charlottenburg was not a completely safe place. Soviet agents tried to kidnap Ingrid Hoeck and her children to pressure Horst Hoeck to return to the Soviet zone and face trial. Luckily, they did not succeed. But the Hoecks got the message. They decided Ingrid and her children would move to Bavaria while Karin, the daughter from Horst's first marriage, was sent to a children's home by the North Sea. Horst Hoeck remained alone in Berlin. Not only did he suffer from his injuries, but had to work hard to accept the new circumstances. Erich Emanuel, his general manager, had done a good job in difficult times. Hoeck took stock: the front building was more or less okay. Ricochets had damaged the tapping system and some shelves, but everything still worked. However, the offices

in the rear building as well as the basement with the distilling facilities had been destroyed by a bomb.

There was no chance to restart the distillery to prewar volume. Furthermore, raw materials were scarce and the British occupiers only allowed production for personal consumption. Luckily, that included operating the pub, which had remained open throughout the war. And more than ever you heard: *It is always time for a drink.*

Around 1950, Horst Hoeck had recovered from most of his injuries and brought his daughter Karin back to Berlin. In 1952, Ingrid and Horst Hoeck separated and divorced. Meanwhile, the economy had gained momentum: the tavern and the wine store prospered, and contracts for filling bottles flooded the coffers. But there was competition on the horizon: bottling machines worked faster and cheaper, Hoeck no longer was able to compete. He had to think of something new.

In 1954, he closed the wine store to reopen as a restaurant with home-style cooking. The *Berliner Kindl* brewing company, a partner since his father opened the tavern, financially supported the necessary construction work that included incorporating the former hall into the new restaurant. A special feature of the restaurant was the foldaway front window, which added a beer garden feeling. Unfortunately, the mechanism was temperamental. In the early 70s, the window twisted beyond repair and had to be reverted to a normal shop window.

Hoeck's idea turned out to be brilliant: right from the start employees from stores and companies around, clerks

Restaurant (1954)

from the town hall nearby as well as the stage crew from the opera house were regular guests for lunch. In those days a beer or two during working hours was permitted.

The 50s were the decade of German *Gemutlichkeit*, and what could be more *gemutlich* than a nice old Berlin pub? Almost overnight, Hoeck had become old-fashioned among all the new, stark, modern buildings. Hoeck seemed to be a remnant from the *Kaiser's* Reich. Probably that was exactly the reason why students discovered the place in the 60s. *Wilhelm Hoeck 1892* simply was too old to have any Nazi history. And Horst Hoeck, the athlete and Olympic champion, was above reproach. Anyway, the tavern was not too far away from Berlin's *Technische Universität*. And it offered food and drinks at reasonable prices.

The 60s were the decade of earnest discussions as well as outrageous nonsense. *Hoeck* was a place for both. The young crowd discussed world changes for hours and hours, and they pelted each other with teabags. Every now and then someone threw a bag up to the ceiling, where it stuck for a while, until gravity pulled it down again. There was one exception: one of the bags has been stuck there for several decades and still can be admired. Rumor has it, the bag was thrown by Rudi Dutschke, leader of the German student movement in the late 60s.

Horst Hoeck passed away April 12, 1969. His third wife Hildegard, whom he had married in 1967, appointed Erich Emanuel general manager. But he was nearly 60 years old and planned to retire in 1972, after 50 years in the *Hoeck* company. So, Hildegard Hoeck had to look for replacement. She never had attended to business; that had always been her husband's concern. On the other hand, she felt too old to train and above all trust a new manager. So, she decided to lease the pub and the restaurant out in 1972.

Peter Dahms was the first leaseholder. As butcher and head of a lunchroom he was attracted to the idea of man-

Peter Dahms (Leaseholder 1972 – 1993)

aging a restaurant on his own. He soon found out, that the tavern was a virtual gold mine. 40 years after the founder's death, Hoeck's spirit still was around, and Dahms was willing to continue the tradition. He was in charge until 1993.

His successor was Holger Wiedenhöft, who had joined the team in 1989. In his first year, history was in the making.

In the summer of '89, the people of the *German Democratic Republic* openly opposed their government. Resentments grew to protest, which cumulated in the Monday marches in Leipzig and other East German cities. Surrounded by East Germany, West Berlin was especially attuned by the political rumblings. The *Hoeck* regulars started to meet daily instead of once a week and exchanged the latest news. Almost everyone had friends or relatives on the other side of the Berlin Wall and could add information. Excitement was in the air, and nobody knew where it was leading.

On the evening of November 9, the Berlin Wall opened; it was not too long before the first guests from the East entered *Hoeck*. The stream of visitors went on and on the next days. Then the direction changed, and the West Berliners discovered the East, fueled by the unofficial exchange rate of 1:10 making evenings there very cheap. Everything was new and exciting. That meant bad times for West Berlin's gastronomy. Only after the economy and currency union of July 1990 did the situation normalize again.

In 1992, *Hoeck* celebrated its centennial and everybody joined the party. The mayor, the chairman of the guild, the CEO of the *Berliner Kindl* brewery and honored guests from the *Hotel & Restaurant Association* were official well-wishers, followed by regular and irregular guests. Beer was for free, but everybody had to buy a commemorative beer mug. Proceeds from the sale were donated to a senior citizens home in the East Berlin district of *Köpenick*.

One year, later Pater Dahms passed the lease over to Holger Wiedenhöft. Even after one hundred years *Hoeck* was going strong. But in 1998 the whole industry fell into a crisis. The *Hotel & Restaurant Association* predicted the closing of about 1,000 pubs. The number of guests decreased, turnover dropped, young people developed a new enter-

Holger Wiedenhöft (Leaseholder 1993 – 2010)

tainment culture with stylish lounges, cool bars or event gastronomy. Cocktails and long drinks were on the rise, beer
consumption declined. But Wiedenhöft could count on his
regulars who remained loyal to *Wilhelm Hoeck 1892*.

Hildegard Hoeck passed away at the end of 2000, her step-
daughter Karin Isermann from Horst's first marriage being

the sole heiress. She was determined to keep her grand-father's and her father's heritage alive as family enterprise. So, everything stayed the way it was. And the next anniversary was just around the corner. 2003 the company celebrated its 111th birthday, and again everybody was invited. Beer and schnapps were sold for 1,11 mark each. In recognition of the 1992 donation, the Berlin district of *Köpenick* sent his famous *Hauptmann von Köpenick* (Captain of Köpenick). This character recalls of a brash fraud that took place in 1906:

Wilhelm Voigt was a poor shoemaker who never found his place in society, after released from prison. He did not get a passport, so he could not get a job or a place to live. In abject despair he disguised as an army captain, organized a couple of obedient soldiers, occupied the Köpenick city hall, arrested the mayor and stole the city treasury. Of course he got caught, but the Köpenick officials became a butt of jokes for their gullibility.

The actor, who starred as the *Hauptmann von Köpenick* at the 2003 *Hoeck* jubilee, did not steal anything, not even a glass of beer. On the contrary: his performance was rewarded with amusement, laughter and a long applause.

The successors of Horst Hoeck, though, were not amused by Hildegard Hoeck's last will. Karin Isermann as sole heiress had to give in. In order to settle all claims she had to sell the building including the tavern that carried her grandfather's name in 2005. A Bavarian couple became the new owners.

Holger Wiedenhöft, who had been leaseholder since 1993, retired 2010 and handed the pub and restaurant over to Berlin businessman Hagen Müller. After his death in 2012 his daughter Tanja stepped into the contract for the five consequent years. The new leaseholders Marko and Eiko were immediately impressed by the history of the location. They quietly and carefully renewed all technical installations and remodeled the restaurant in the best

Berlin tradition, including a typical Berlin cuisine at reasonable prices, introducing »Berliner Happen«, a collection of tapas-like Berlin specialities to enjoy either as starter or as a square meal. It sure is worth tasting.

The remodeling was finished shortly before the 125th anniversary of *Wilhelm Hoeck 1892*, which was celebrated a whole weekend in June 2017. Now, this unique place will remain as a second living room for regulars, tourists and friends. It is a place of authentic ambiance, where they all can raise a glass to tradition and to Horst Hoeck, the Olympic champion.

The 2017 remodeled »Berlin Style« restaurant

Impressions of the anniversary celebrations: The »Artistocraten« enthuse the guests with a spectacular performance.

TWELVE INCHES FROM VICTORY

It was pinned to the wall in 1932, and ever since it was proof of a career crowned by glory: the certificate of Horst Hoeck's gold medal in the coxed four at the 1932 Olympic

Games in Los Angeles. For many years, the medal itself seemed lost, but in 2015 it reappeared quite sensationally. But reducing Horst Hoeck to this one victory champion means to diminish this enthusiastic and successful athlete.

Shortly after Hoeck started to row, he joined the Berlin Rowing-Club in 1925, a club with a long tradition located at the banks of the *Wannsee* lake. His trainer Tom Sullivan, an amateur in rowing and sculling from New Zealand who later turned professional, soon detected the potential of 21-year old Horst and suggested that he start in three boat classes. And Sullivan proved to be correct. Only a year later, in 1926, Horst Hoeck collected fourteen victories in single sculls, double sculls and coxed eight, the brass ring of rowing. He defended most of his victories in 1927 and

was sent to the Olympic Games in Amsterdam in 1928, where unfortunately he did not make the finals.

After two years in South America with his sister Ilse's family, he returned to Berlin and to the sculls. In 1931, he won another German championship in the coxed eight. Due to an incapacitated rower in the coxed four, Horst helped out on short notice in that class, winning a second championship. Although the Berliner RC boat missed the 1932 qualification, the German Olympic Committee decided to send the boat to Los Angeles. Due to the worldwide economic crisis, the German team numbered only 83 athletes. And these competitors even had to travel to Los Angeles on their own expenses. Horst Hoeck and his team departed from Berlin for a six weeks journey by railroad and ocean liner to California.

However, the odds were not in their favor. The Italian boat was the outstanding favorite, the German team had to compete against them in the preliminary heat. Other contenders were New Zealand and Brazil. Germany came in second, only by a split second after the winning Italians. At least they qualified for the repechage. New Zealand took first, while the German boat again took second, thus qualifying for the final. And again it was the Italian boat they hat to compete against. The Southern Europeans were confident of their victory. An eyewitness described the final race with rampant emotions:

»Rarely before has a race been turned around like this. About two hundred yards to the finish, the Italians still led by a length, their victory being only a matter of form. With an unprecedented burst of energy, the German boat approached the competitor inch by inch. Desperately, the Italians in their light blue jerseys put up a fight, but their lead became smaller and smaller. A few powerful strokes by the Germans, and both the boats shot over the finish line,

»Germany's finest victory«, read the caption ...

... in the 1932 Olympic Games Collector's Album
published by cigarette maker Reemtsma in October 1932

the Germans apparently with few inches ahead. The excitement was immense, the phenomenal final spurt had impressed enormously. Moments of anxious waiting passed by slowly as the judges debated the matter. When Germany was officially announced Olympic champion, an overwhelming applause swelled to praise the magnificent performance by the Germans, who presented themselves in front of the grandstands in admirable freshness. It was a splendid performance. Wherever the Germans showed up, they were overwhelmed with applause. Whoever witnessed this victory will never forget it.«

With this unexpected victory, Horst Hoeck and his team contributed one of the five gold medals to the 1932 German medal count, which also included twelve silver and five bronze medals. Compared to 1928, the result was devastating; in Amsterdam, the German team then had collected ten golden, seven silver and fourteen bronze medals.

A column of honor, located at the Berlin Olympic Stadium, names all ten German 1932 gold medal winners. These are the five athletes in the coxed four: Hans Eller, Horst Hoeck (long pants), Walter Meyer, Joachim Spremberg and Carlheinz Neumann (photo) as well as Rudolf Ismayer (weight lifting) and Jacob Brendel (wrestling Greek-Roman style).

Further gold medals went to Franz and Toni Schmidt (alpinists) and Paul Bauer for his book about the Himalaya tours in 1929 and 1931. Few people recall that between 1912 and 1948 the Olympic disciplines included the competition in fine arts (architecture, sculpting, literature, painting and music), as long as there was a reference to sports, of course.

Sadly, the German public did not give the 1932 victory much recognition. At least the certificate and an original scull from the winning boat keep the memory alive, although it is not Horst Hoeck's original scull. That one was stolen in the 1960s, probably by an unscrupulous memorabilia collector. Since then, the wall in the tavern is decorated with another scull from the 1932 boat. It belonged to Horst Eller, who was missing in action from the WW II Eastern Front since 1943.

The discovery of the long lost gold medal form 1932 was almost as sensational as the victory itself. It all started in a day care center at Kleinmachnow, a suburb of Berlin, that was in the need of being redeveloped in 2015. When construction workers tore down a wall that was not in the construction plans, they found a hidden wall with a safe in it. The workers wanted to uncover treasure, but there was no key. So, they had to crack the safe, but that was easier said than done. It took some time until the heavy steel door opened with a groan. A flashlight illuminated the interior, but the old safe seemed to be empty. The workers were crestfallen. But one of them did not give up. Again and again, he illuminated every inch of the old safe, when finally he discovered something in the back corner. He retrieved the *something* with his strong hands; it was a small box. He opened the lid, and all the workers held their breath. The box contained a gold medal from the Olympic Games 1932 in Los Angeles.

But who could be the owner? And were there any heirs? These questions sprung to mind. The director of the day

care center started to research and discovered the victory of the coxed four of the Berliner Rowing Club. But there was no clue to whether any one of the athletes had ever lived at this particular address. The municipal directories solely recorded a certain Werner Brune as owner, who owned the building between 1930 and 1948. But he did not have any connections to the rowing club or its members. Some more research revealed a clue to the puzzle.

After Horst Hoeck had married his second wife in 1942, he started to work as a director in his father-in-law's business *Bio-Malz* in Teltow outside of Berlin. Shortly afterwards, he rented the *Kleinmachnow* house and moved there with his family. The 1932 gold medal was put in the safe. But Hoeck's imprisonment in 1947 and his sensational rescue a few of weeks later left Ingrid Hoeck little time to organize the escape from the Soviet Occupation Zone. At the time, the gold medal was the least important thing on her mind ...

After the war, the building where the Hoeck family had lived, became state-owned property and later a state-owned day care center. With the end of the Socialist regime, the building passed to public authorities. Some time between 1947 and 2015, the second wall in the living room was built, effectively hiding the safe with the gold medal. But no one remembered the fact or the date. That is why the discovery was such a sensation.

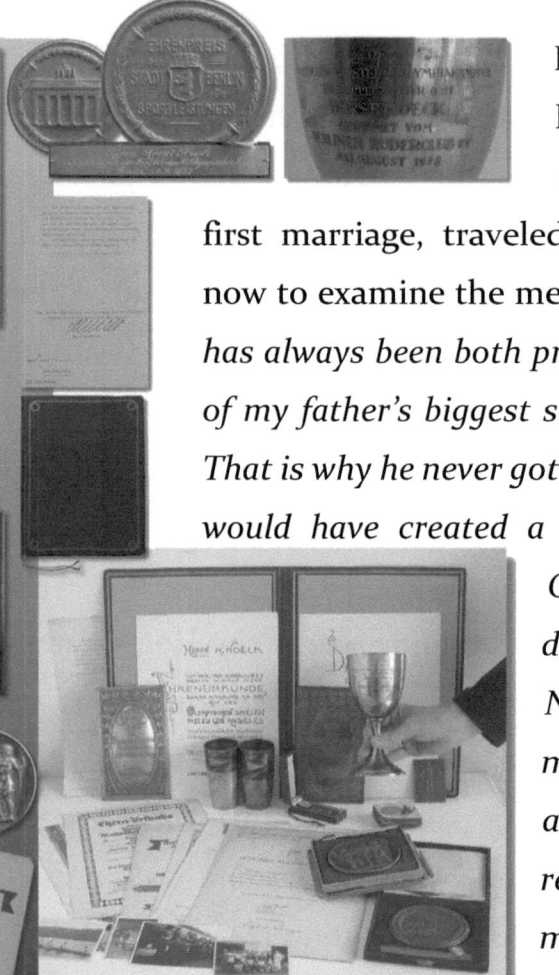

Karin Isermann, Horst Hoeck's daughter from his first marriage, traveled to Kleinmachnow to examine the medal: »*This medal has always been both proof and memory of my father's biggest success in sports. That is why he never got over the loss. He would have created a replica, but the Olympic Statutes did not allow that. Now I will take the medal to his grave and tell him, it has returned to the family.*«

Some of Hoerst Hoeck's sports memorabilia (auction catalogue)

The city of Kleinmachnow will honor the Olympic champion with a permanent exhibition in the local museum. Karin Isermann has agreed to contribute a replica of the medal. And she will visit the day care center to tell the children about her father's life, which includes not only sports, but history also.

The Olympic certificate and the corresponding gold medal are the only tangible memories left of an exciting athletic career. All the other trophies and awards, which were once displayed in the tavern, disappeared in mysterious ways and re-emerged in 2014, when they were bought at an auction by an anonymous sport fan abroad.

SPOTTING REGULARS

They step in, look around, – and breathe a sigh of relief that obviously nothing has changed; men and women who return to Berlin after ten, twenty or even fifty years to look for their memories, and they find them all at the *Hoeck* tavern. Time seems to stand still in the Berlin-Charlottenburg's oldest pub thanks to the founder.

Hoeck regulars are not just people who want to drink a beer and meet friends. *Hoeck* regulars are captivated by the history of the place, and this feeling never stops – even when they leave Berlin for another city. The world may change, but *Hoeck* does not, and the regulars know what to expect. Some could possibly have known the founder himself, since they have been coming to *Hoeck* regularly for fifty or more years. On the other hand, the young crowd that started to populate *Hoeck* in the last years, proves the irresistible attraction of the patina of time, smoke and beer.

Nevertheless, even the regulars are different. Some meet every week and remember the olden days. Others just finish their day's work with a beer or two. Or look at the businessman who celebrates a contract with his partners or invites his clients to the taste of Berlin-style cuisine like cabbage roll, pork shank or a typical sausage in curry sauce. You'll also find the Berlin tourist who has succumbed to this place's charms, or the senior citizen who prefers company over the loneliness of his apartment. And sometimes you may meet a German actor or a former Berlin mayor. Although they are celebrities, they are just guests; they walk in and enjoy the *Hoeck* normality.

Nothing has changed since the beginning. When Wilhelm Hoeck owned the place, laborers came in after work for their share of beer and schnapps before they went home for supper. If they wanted to finish the day with a last beer, they would send over their offspring to buy beer in a siphon to keep the carbonation. This offspring eventually became regulars; a perfect way to perpetuate with success.

In the old days, there were few options how to pass leisure time: vacation was almost unknown to the working class, radio broadcasts did not start before 1925, a visit to the movie theaters was expensive, and television had not been invented yet. Even the *Kurfürstendamm*, center of entertainment located at the other end of the *Wilmersdorfer Straße*, was a world too strange and far away. There was nothing else than to go to the pub around the corner, which was like a second living room.

When Horst Hoeck took over the helm in 1933, the regulars accepted him from the first moment on. He used to run around the tables as a little boy; he was a member of the family and had been a successful athlete.

But when his widow leased the pub and the restaurant to Peter Dahms in 1972, the regulars were sceptical. Could he run this particular place, maintain the special atmosphere? At the beginning, he had a hard time; everything he did and said, was compared to Wilhelm and Horst Hoeck. But with a well-established team he succeeded in inspiring confidence that everything would stay as it was.

In the early 1970s, there were some regulars who were the same age as *Hoeck*. Their fathers had sent them for beer, later they downed a beer after work, and now as retirees they come in every morning at nine o'clock to spend some time with friends, exchanging old stories and playing cards. The more they play, the more they drink, and it does not take too long until they rant and rave about a lost card game and leave the pub. But that does not hinder them from returning the next morning – and everything starts all over again. It is an amusing spectacle every day.

Over the years, life has changed for senior citizens. There are other ways to pass the time than in a pub. So their visits become rare. Nevertheless, Peter Dahms still can rely on a huge number of regulars. *Wilhelm Hoeck 1892* still is the top establishment in the area; every now and then a new pub starts to challenge the claim, but no one ever succeeds in displacing *Hoeck*. It has become an institution with four stable cornerstones: tradition, quality, reliability and atmosphere. The clientele knows what to expect – and that is exactly what they get.

Why should it change, when Holger Wiedenhöft took over in 1993? He had already been a member of the *Hoeck* team for four years and knew his peers thoroughly. He talked to those who were looking for distraction, and left those alone who came for a break. This is why there is no TV set, except for soccer championships. Music is kind of hand-made: the *Hoeck* guests prefer the good old jukebox with songs from the good old days. And they enjoy the communicative atmosphere: people who have never met start to talk to each other, regardless of their age, profession or *Weltanschauung*. That makes *Hoeck* a favorite place not only for people from the neighborhood, but also guests come from across town. And that is what turns visitors to regulars. Some of them have found their place in the tavern's history; they have become *Hoeck* archetypes.

Let's take a look at some regulars. Similarities with today's guest are a mere coincidence ... or what do you think?

At first: Richard. Nobody knew his last name, but that did not make a difference. A first name or a nickname was enough. Richard was short and stocky and wore his hair carefully slicked back with Brill cream. When Peter Dahms, the leaseholder, met him for the first time in 1972, he found out, Richard was 80 years old, thus being as old as the tavern itself. He grew up and lived around the corner; and was a regular as his father had already been. Richard came from a time when families had to pinch pennies, that is why he was thrifty. Some people would call it even being cheap, but Richard's pension was not that meager. For a long time, he worked as custodian in a Charlottenburg school. He was responsible for cleaning and taking care of everything as well as disciplining pupils with truant behavior. Obviously, the students did not like him, so they called him *watchdog* and *killjoy*. But Richard loved his job that allowed him to be strict and pedantic. Even years after retirement he weighed everyone's word, and the other regulars were very careful not to get his nose out of joint. He stepped into *Hoeck* every morning at nine o'clock, dead on time, and sat in the same chair at the same table every day. Right away he ordered a small glass of wine. He set the topics to be discussed. After all, he never had hesitated to contradict the school principal. But his topics were all the same: money, money, money, be it the costs of living or price increases. He did not even spare *Hoeck*, although the prices there had stayed the same. Occasionally somebody interrupted his litany offering to buy him another glass of wine, which he generously accepted. Around noon his wife called for lunch, and he left, or better: after six or seven glasses of wine he more or less staggered out of the pub, still complaining about the prices. But actually, he had been invited to most of the drinks; he only paid for the first one himself.

Or have a look at Erich, the blacksmith. He really was quite unique at about six feet six tall, heavily built with a  broad back, strawberry blond hair and funny freckles all over. In his youth, he had been a blacksmith and at seventy, he was still a fine figure of a man. He was the total opposite of Richard: he barely spoke, and he preferred beer over wine. But every now and then somebody asked him: »*Erich, please do that again, will you?*«. And then he rose slowly and silently, grabbed two chairs by their leg, one in each hand, and lifted them slowly and almost gracefully and balanced the chairs with extended arms for several minutes. Then, he set them back on the ground, sat down again and quietly enjoyed the attention and the applause.

Or think of *Kohlen-Ernst (Ernest, the coal-miner)*: His nickname was a relict of days gone by. In fact, he had never worked in a coal mine, but had delivered coal to households for many years. When the central heating replaced the coal ovens, he had to change jobs and so he signed on with a moving company close to the *Charlottenburg Palace*. And he really looked like he  could carry heavy weights even if it was 60 lbs. of coal or an old piano. His massive physique commanded the

respect of his counterparts, even awed them. But that did not suit Ernst at all, he was too shy to attract attention. When he entered *Hoeck*, he ordered a beer and looked for a place to withdraw to. But after the third *Berliner Kindl* beer he came out of his shell and started to talk to other guests or amused them by telling jokes. At least for a short time he was able to overcome his shyness.

Another one of the senior regulars was called *Herzilein*, which translates to *Sweetheart*. He was part of a regular group who discussed all diseases, ailments and the aches and pains that complicate life. His particular nickname was no coincidence, since *Herzilein* already had survived a heart transplant, making him the undisputed leader of the gang. Regularly he presented his lab results. One fine day, out of the blue, he asked the leaseholder about his state of health, who earnestly declared that he would get his status the following week. That very day the seniors examined the leaseholder's results very thoroughly only to find out with a laugh, that the liver values were way too normal for a bartender. They kept teasing the leaseholder, who got more and more irritated about the accuracy of the results. Finally, he went to see the doctor again – and could breathe a sigh of relief: everything was just fine.

Good memories are connected to *Henkel-Werner*, whose nickname refers to a preferred type of beer glass: the one with a handle. Werner used to work for the Charlottenburg municipal authority, but retired some years ago and moved to another district. But every Friday he stepped into *Hoeck*, just as he had done the last forty years. So he knew a lot of people, chatted here, laughed  there – and in between had his share of beer. Inevitably he reached the moment, when the beer affected his pronunciation and he could no longer speak clearly. At this point he decided to take a cab home. But that was easier said than done, because the cab driver could not understand Werner's address. So the leaseholder had to take over: »*Werner, where do you want to go to?*«. Werner's answer was garbled, but the leaseholder understood and told the puzzled cab driver the complete address including street and number.

Another famous guest was *Karl*, who lived just two blocks away. Whenever he stepped into *Hoeck*, he was dressed to the nines and carried a fine black briefcase tucked under his left arm. He sure looked like a successful businessman until the moment he had the famous one beer too many. Karl tried very hard not to show his inebriation, but his off-balance movements gave him away. Even fresh air outside did not sober him up, and he unsteadily made his his way home weaving from side to side along the sidewalk.

And last, but not least, the leaseholder remembers the young couple that stepped in one morning at eight o'clock.

The doors had just opened, but the early guests must have been out all night. Now they needed an early morning nightcap. The leaseholder drew two beer and left for the kitchen to prepare for the day. When he returned to the restaurant, he found both the glasses and the table empty. Seemingly, the early couple had left the pub without paying for the beer. The leaseholder was hopping mad. But when he passed the restrooms, he heard unusual but rhythmic noise. Not too much later the young people returned to their table, but the leaseholder shook his head in disapproval. That prompted the young man to step up to the counter. »*There is nothing wrong with some fun in the morning*«, he said – well, he said a bit differently, and ordered two more beers.

All the men and women who have been regulars, have one thing in common: they lived happily ever after ... at least in the memory and the history of Charlottenburg's oldest tavern, *Wilhelm Hoeck 1892*.

HEINRICH ZILLE –
THE SHARP-WITTED OBSERVER

Heinrich Zille.

If there is one Berlin artist who really cared about the ordinary Joe, it was Heinrich Zille. He was a famous painter and sharp-witted observer, who lived from 1858 to 1929. As most of the *typical* Berlin celebrities, he was not born in the Prussian capital. He grew up in a Saxon village by the name of *Radeburg*, not too far from Dresden, and moved to Berlin with his parents in 1867. Actually, the family had to leave their hometown head over heels. Zille's father, a watchmaker, managed his money badly, and could not pay his debts. But the streets of Berlin were not plastered with gold, either. Until 1872, the family had to live in a wretched basement hovel.

Zille's teachers discovered his talent and his enthusiasm for drawing and encouraged him to become a lithographer. His father was more practical. Heinrich Zille served his apprenticeship in a butcher shop because that meant there would always be enough to eat. But Heinrich could not stand the sight of blood. So, he began with lithographic studies and took additional courses at the *Berlin Royal School of Arts*. He finished in 1875 and started to work for several companies. In 1877, he was admitted to the *Photographic Society* where he was introduced to new reproduction techniques. He would be a member of the Society for thirty years. In the 1880s, he started to capture his impressions of rear-yards, side streets and working class places with crayons and camera, thus creating a style of his own that would make him famous. But not everybody was eager to be confronted with the unmasked poverty in the streets of the German capital. Visitors to his first exhibition in 1901 rendered an annihilating judgment: he was accused of robbing everyone's pleasure in life. Maybe the visitors to the exhibition preferred to close their eyes and conscience to the squalor and poverty in the city.

Wilhelm II, the German emperor, even called his work *curbstone art*. But Zille kept his tail up. He modified his work and added black humor thus creating the style he is famous for today. Then he painted crazy guys and curvaceous women, lame ducks and underdogs, and children from the underclass – a winking inventory of reality.

In 1892, Heinrich Zille moved to Charlottenburg's *Sophie-Charlotte-Straße*, only a couple of blocks away from Wilhelm Hoeck's newly started business. In 1907, he was ousted from the *Photographic Society*, which made him quite angry. By then, he was so well known that he dared to go on as a freelance artist. He looked for themes on his own and painted on commission. In 1916, he finished a drawing called *Schnapsdestille* (distillery), which certainly was in-

Schnaps destille.

Schnapsgewordnes Elend hockt in der Destille,
Wo giftiger Brodem klebt.
Hier will es ertränken,
Was trübes Gedenken
Die Erinnerung webt.

Die Lampe dreht sich wie ein Karussel.
Die Gläser tanzen. Weiber keifen.
Schnäpse funkeln und lachen grell.
Sauf nur Gesell,
Willst du das Leben begreifen.

Schmierige Groschen singen Bettellieder.
Und Muttertränen wimmern in der Luft
Vom Hunger, der die Kinder krallt.
Die Augen stieren aus ihrer Gruft
Und die Seele schluchzt
Bis sie trunken ist
Und lallt.

Bruno Schönlank

fluenced by the *Hoeck* interior, such as the kegs, the bottles, the watch and the furniture. Zille had been a guest of many bars, but he rather observed than drank. His unerring eye, uncompromising style and excellent technique finally made him a member of the Academy of Arts in 1924. In the same year, he was appointed professor.

The people of Berlin, who had taken him into their hearts, kept on calling him *Pinsel-Heinrich* (»Paintbrush-Heinrich«), which he took as a badge of honor. When he passed away in 1929, about two thousand mourners followed the funeral procession. In 1947, a street close to *Wilhelm Hoeck 1892* was named after him, and in 1992, finally, Heinrich Zille was made an Honorary Citizen of Berlin.

TRADITION AT ITS BEST

At *Wilhelm Hoeck 1892* tradition is not just a phrase. The tavern has lovingly cared for its special atmosphere and patina. Upon entering, one's glance first falls on the wooden kegs with their small brass taps preserved over the decades by tobacco smoke. Until 1933, the kegs were filled

with schnapps and liquors to be decanted before being sold to customers. Since then, they make wonderful curiosity objects. The wall on the left hand presents a gallery of old *Hoeck*-products. The cabinets testify to the fine craftsmanship at the turn of the century. The eyes wander over old and

well-preserved bottles that once contained the homemade schnapps and liqueurs bearing names of mostly long-forgotten varieties, such as *Pfefferminz grün* (peppermint), *Halb und Halb* (made half from herbs and half from bitter orange), *Bergamotte* (bergamot), *Cherry Brandy*, *Reiterlikör* (orange flavored cordial), *Blutorange* (blood orange) and *Ananas* (pine-apple) liqueur, *Magenlikör* (bitter) and *Berliner Kümmel* (caraway). All these varieties attest to the inventiveness of Wilhelm Hoeck, who actually distilled almost everything he found in nature.

The wall on the right seems like a liquor dealer's showcase. Brands and varieties from the 1950s and 1960s alternate with all the current drinks on the menu. The shelves were damaged in World War II; the bullet holes can still be seen on the tapping system. Further along the shelves, the eyes rest on strange-looking bottles with four small tubes around the body. They are called *Gluckerflaschen* (gurgle bottles) due to the specific sound that is produced when pouring. They contain colorful liquids, but unfit for consumption. Gossip has it that the liquid is only colored water.

Apropos colored water: The *Hoeck* private label schnapps used to shimmer light yellow because it was an unfiltered grain alcohol. So, everybody just ordered *a yellow one*.

Horst Hoeck had to close down the distillery in the early 1950s, due to damage from bombing during the war. So, he and his successors had to

source the »yellow« schnapps from other distilleries. But over time, the number of distilleries decreased, until only one provider was left, who of course steadily increased the price. In order to save money, the leaseholder decided to buy clear schnapps by the keg, which was less expensive,

and added just a few drops of caramel color for distinctive light yellow tint. And nobody noticed the difference ...

Talking about prices directly leads to the normal end of a pleasant stay: the moment, when the guest is asked to settle the bill. Nobody likes to spend too much money, but at *Wilhelm Hoeck 1892* even this is completely different. Everybody loves the mighty copper cash register that was manufactured in 1907 by the famous German steelmaker *Krupp*. At least that is what the stamp says, but even long-serving employees cannot remember *Krupp* ever making a product that even resembled a cash register. Nevertheless, it is true. The cash register has more than one hundred years of service, and still works without any problems. Too bad that tax laws require modern electronic cash registers to print sales slips including VAT and more. If you do not need a receipt, the shiny Krupp monster still does duty and adds every single item to your invoice with a bright

chime instead of a soulless rumble. Even the toughest guy gets teary-eyed – like a child at Christmas time – at the sound of the merry chime. So celebrate the good old hardware with an extra beer and a smile!

What good is a celebration without music? At *Wilhelm Hoeck 1892*, the good old jukebox is ready for your selection. Eighty forty-fives with a good mixture from German hits and international standards suit every music taste. But some of the buttons are unlabeled, because the records are meant to surprise the guests. Every now and then, a member of the staff switches out the re-

cords for present rarities or funny songs from the past. Sometimes, though, even a jukebox needs a break, and music is played from a computer playlist. Every now and then street musicians come in to entertain the guests. But it has to be *Hoeck* style to fit in.

Since the mid 1970s, *Wilhelm Hoeck 1892* has become a sought-after location for television and movie productions. It all started with a 13-part TV series, *Ein Mann will nach oben*, after a novel by German writer Hans Fallada, which is a Berlin version of the American dream set in the early 20th century and telling a typical Berlin story. So, the production company needed a typical Berlin tavern. Although the novel takes place in another district of Berlin, the location scout spontaneously knew he had found the right place when he discovered *Hoeck*.

A couple of years later, another TV series, *Jakob und Adele*, was shot at *Hoeck*. It is about two senior citizens who meet by chance in a pub, which becomes their favorite hangout, and discover that life is not over once you have retired and that age is a secondary question, as this snippet of dialogue shows:

»How old are you?«

»Just call me Methuselah's father«.

Since then, millions of people have been to *Hoeck*, if not in person, then at least through television or the movies. No matter if it is a TV series, a crime thriller or the screen adaption of literature, *Hoeck* is the one and only authentic location. In 2008, Italian-American actor Bud Spencer and *Hoeck* starred in the crime comedy *Mord ist mein Geschäft, Liebling* (»Killing Is My Business, Honey«). And in 2012 *The Cloud Atlas* was shot at *Hoeck*, starring Tom Hanks, Hale Berry, Susan Sarandon, Hugh Grant and other fine actors.

To this day, *Hoeck* is a location for TV productions, although set designers sometimes change reality a little bit. In one episode of a German TV series there is a bus stop in front of the entrance. After the episode had been broadcasted, the bartender pulled a prank on the guests, and asked if they had arrived by public transportation. Those who had watched TV, even some of the regulars, started to believe in a newly opened bus route. Nevertheless, the bus stop was never seen again, although *Hoeck* was the location for scenes in every other episode.

And once there was a thriller set in Frankfurt am Main, a city some 350 miles away from Berlin. In one particular scene, the exterior shots show the inspector parking his car in a Frankfurt street in front of a pub and opening the door. The next scene was filmed inside – but it was not a Frankfurt pub at all, but *Hoeck*, where the inspector talked to a witness. When finished, he turned around, was about to leave and – cut! – was back in the Frankfurt street.

1960s

1970s

1983

2008

THE TASTE OF BERLIN

If Germany is well known for anything, it is the broad variety of bread and beer. With regards to the latter, most people think of Bavarian beer as served at the *Oktoberfest*. But Berlin also has its own long brewing tradition.

Since the Early Middle Ages beer has been a nutritional staple. Old certificates indicate that nuns from the Berlin *Convent of the Holy Spirit* brewed a kind of stout in 1288. Several centuries earlier, monks already had devoted themselves intensely to brewing, because it was nutritious and savory, and was permitted during the fasting. *Liquida non frangunt ieunum* – or: Liquid does not break the fast. In fact, the consumption of beer in monasteries took on surprising dimensions; chronicles report that monks were allowed to drink five liters of beer per day.

A quote from 1593 states that brewing was only allowed if a person owned a house and had paid for the legal permit. That way the guilds ensured the craft of brewing remained a secret of a select few. But the municipal authorities soon discovered that the more permits they issued, the more revenue they generated. At first, brewing was only allowed for domestic use, but when the permit holders started to sell beer to neighbors and foreigners, the authorities soon levied a sales tax, which was even more lucrative for the city coffers than just selling permits. Beer started its triumphal procession throughout Berlin.

A typical specialty is the *Berliner Weisse*, a cloudy, sour, white beer, refined with a shot of raspberry (red) or woodruff (green) syrup. This is not to be confused with the similar-sounding Bavarian Weiss beer, which has a different fermentation process. The *Berliner Weisse* is first mentioned in Hamburg around 1642, but it has been known in Berlin since 1572. During the 18th century, it started to be promoted to be <u>the</u> Berlin beer. Due to the refreshing taste, it soon got the nickname *cold brewski*. Napoleon's troops that occupied Prussia in the early 19th century, liked *Berliner Weisse* so much, they called it »*Champagne of the North*«. There are many ways to enjoy the *Berliner Weisse*: with a shot of schnapps it is called *Strippe,* with a blend of champagne or cassis-de-Dijon it is ennobled to be a *Weisse Royal.* Some doctors even recommend a hot Weiss bier with lemon juice to cure a cold.

Around 1800, Berlin counts 172,000 inhabitants, and approximately 700 *Weissbier* taverns. Breweries spring up like mushrooms: the number rises from 74 to 125 between 1820 and 1900. That certainly must make people happy; Benjamin Franklin, one of America's Founding Fathers, is reported to have said: »*Beer is proof that God loves us and wants us to be happy.*« To be honest, he said that about wine, but why shouldn't it apply for beer, too?

Brewing yeasts are traditionally classed as *top-cropping* (or *top-fermenting*) and *bottom-cropping* (or *bottom-fermenting*). Historically, top-fermenting was the more common method to brew beer because it could be done at room temperature. But its shelf life was short. Bottom-fermenting yeast required a brewing temperature below 9° C or 48° F. So, climate, weather or specialized facilities determined if bottom-fermented beer were brewed and stored. This did not change until 1873, when German entrepreneur and inventor Carl Linde developed the industrial ice-making machine.

Since the 16th century Berlin brewers produced top-fermented beer, while Bavarian brewers preferred bottom-fermented ones. No wonder, Bavarian winters are long and cold. Therefore, bottom-fermented beer was often called *Bavarian Beer*. But when this art of brewing came to Prussia in mid 19th century, it was rather called *Pilsener* or *Pils*, after the Bohemian city of Pilsen, southeast of Bavaria, where *bottom-fermented* beer was refined.

Around 1830, a new and strong beer came in town, the *bock beer*. It was supposed to have been a Bavarian invention, but originated in Lower Saxony. Already in 1420, breweries in the city of Einbeck (between Göttingen and Hildesheim) started to produce of a top-fermented beer that sold well beyond the city limits. To survive the transport, the beer had to be brewed to be very strong, thus with high alcohol content. Even the Bavarian dukes enjoyed *Bockbier*, although if it was very expensive. So in 1589, Bavarian Duke *Wilhelm V* decided to headhunt two master brewers from Einbeck and put them to work brewing *bock beer* in a newly built Munich brewery, the *Hof-*

bräuhaus. Due to the regional dialect, the name gradually changed from *Einbecker Bier* to *Bockbier*. The menu in German restaurants often offers a sausage called *Bock-wurst* – and there is a connection between *bock beer* and *Bockwurst*. In 1889, **a pub owner from the Berlin district of Kreuzberg** planned to offer his guests a hearty dish with the popular strong Bock beer. He discussed the matter with a befriended butcher. They came up with a boiled seasoned beef sausage and called it *Bockwurst*.

Wilhelm Hoeck 1892 has been selling *Berliner Kindl* beer, a brand introduced in 1872, adopting the Munich city emblem called *Münch-ner Kindl*, but it got its own logo in 1907: an illustration of a little blond boy who cheekily peeks out of a stein, called *Golden Boy*.

Transport of beer then ...

... and now.

Berliner Kindl is one of the three local beer brands remaining in Berlin today. Apart from a huge variety of international beers, from as far as Australia, South America or China, a few microbreweries have sprung up in the German capital. They produce Craft Beer or *Kiezbier* – a beer from the neighborhood – that is manufactured in the best tradition of proven and tested craftsmanship and sold in the bars and pubs around. So, whatever type or brand of beer you might prefer: it always will be the taste of Berlin.

FINALLY ...

Now the excursion through the history of Charlottenburg, *Wilhelm Hoeck 1892* and the Berlin beer history has come to an end. In case you liked it, please do come back and have a beer on the Berlin *Gemuetlichkeit* and the Olympic champion Horst Hoeck. Doing research for this book was a wonderful walk through time. It was a walk through history and presence as well as a walk through rumors and anecdotes. Research made it necessary to spend quite some time at *Wilhelm Hoeck 1892*. It sounds less suspicious if you say: »*I have to do some research*«, instead of admitting you are going for a beer! *Hoeck*, as you have discovered by now, is not just a tavern. It is a special place from the good old days preserved with affection and commitment. I am very grateful to the friendly people who supplied all the old stories and photos and thus have made this book possible:

Karin Isermann and Horst Hoeck jr., Wilhelm Hoeck's grandchildren; Peter Dahms and Holger Wiedenhöft, leaseholders between 1972 and 2010; the staff of the Charlottenburg Museum of Local History and the Berlin Municipal Archive; Martina Bellack, Kleinmachnow Municipal Authority; the *Berliner Kindl* brewery – and especially my dear friend Vivian Romney for her support in, how she put it, trying »*to superimpose a German writing style on an excellent, but non-literary, English and achieve comprehensible English prose*«.

Berlin, August 2018 – Matthias Gerschwitz

PICTURE CREDITS & REFERENCES

Picture Credits (Pages):

M. Gerschwitz: 4, 6, 15, 19 (3), 22 (3), 26, 27, 31, 33, 54, 61, 78/79, 89-93, 94, 95;
K. Isermann/H. Hoeck: 29, 34, 38, 55; **H. Wiedenhöft:** 9, 40, 47, 87, 99 (2);
Bernd Zeller: 71, 74, 76, 77, 81; **Berlin Archives/H. Siegmann:** 45, 47 (2);
Radeberger Group: 105, 108; **Reemtsma:** 58/59; **Wikipedia:** 84;
Museum Charlottenburg-Wilmersdorf: 19 (3), 99 (2), **Museum Neukölln:** 106;
AGON: 66; **G. Gauglitz:** 23, 28; **Kleinmachnow Municipal Authority:** 64;
Pico Risto: 51, 52/53, 78 (u.l.), 79 (u.r.), 107; **ZDF/Barbara Oloffs:** 97; **zeno.org:** 12;

References:

Memories of Karin Isermann, Dr.-Ing. Horst Hoeck, Peter Dahms and Holger Wiedenhöft; Museum Charlottenburg-Wilmersdorf; Evangelische Luisengemeinde Charlottenburg; Publication *100 Years of Berliner Kindl*; Historical Information of the Charlottenburg-Wilmersdorf Authority; Charlottenburg-Wilmersdorf Building Authority, and Newspaper Articles taken from *Potsdamer Neueste Nachrichten* and *Märkische Allgemeine Zeitung* (August 2015). Further references mentioned in the text.